DISRUPTIVE MOOD DYSREGULATION DISORDER JOURNAL FOR PARENTS

DISRUPTIVE MOOD BEHAVIOR ASSESSMENT WORKSHEET

DATE _____

TOP 3 DISRUPTIVE PROBLEMS TODAY

○ _____

○ _____

○ _____

SOLUTION DIAGRAM: _____

HE / SHE MADE ME

Behavioral observations that require continuous follow-up

_____

_____

_____

Suggestions to do

Evaluation of applied treatment ideas

Overall assessment of disruptive mood behavior

☆ ☆ ☆ ☆ ☆

Weekly / Monthly Goals

BEHAVIORAL OBJECTIVES

♡ _____

♡ _____

♡ _____

PARENTAL GOALS

♡ _____

♡ _____

♡ _____

THERAPEUTIC OBJECTIVES

♡ _____

♡ _____

♡ _____

DISRUPTIVE MOOD BEHAVIOR ASSESSMENT WORKSHEET

DATE _____

TOP 3 DISRUPTIVE PROBLEMS TODAY

_____
○
_____
○
_____
○
_____

SOLUTION DIAGRAM: _____

HE / SHE MADE ME

Behavioral observations that require continuous follow-up

_____

_____

_____

_____

Suggestions to do

Evaluation of applied treatment ideas

Overall assessment of disruptive mood behavior

☆ ☆ ☆ ☆ ☆

Weekly Monthly Goals

BEHAVIORAL OBJECTIVES

♡ _____

♡ _____

♡ _____

PARENTAL GOALS

♡ _____

♡ _____

♡ _____

THERAPEUTIC OBJECTIVES

♡ _____

♡ _____

♡ _____

DISRUPTIVE MOOD BEHAVIOR ASSESSMENT WORKSHEET

DATE _____

TOP 3 DISRUPTIVE PROBLEMS TODAY

○ _____

○ _____

○ _____

HE / SHE MADE ME

Behavioral observations that require continuous follow-up

SOLUTION DIAGRAM: _____

_____

_____

_____

Suggestions to do

Evaluation of applied treatment ideas

Overall assessment of disruptive mood behavior

☆ ☆ ☆ ☆ ☆

Weekly / Monthly Goals

BEHAVIORAL OBJECTIVES

♡ _____

♡ _____

♡ _____

PARENTAL GOALS

♡ _____

♡ _____

♡ _____

THERAPEUTIC OBJECTIVES

♡ _____

♡ _____

♡ _____

DISRUPTIVE MOOD BEHAVIOR ASSESSMENT WORKSHEET

DATE _____

TOP 3 DISRUPTIVE PROBLEMS TODAY

○ _____

○ _____

○ _____

SOLUTION DIAGRAM: _____

HE / SHE MADE ME

Behavioral observations that require continuous follow-up

_____

_____

_____

_____

Suggestions to do

Evaluation of applied treatment ideas

Overall assessment of disruptive mood behavior

☆ ☆ ☆ ☆ ☆

Weekly Monthly Goals

BEHAVIORAL OBJECTIVES

♡ _____

♡ _____

♡ _____

PARENTAL GOALS

♡ _____

♡ _____

♡ _____

THERAPEUTIC OBJECTIVES

♡ _____

♡ _____

♡ _____

DISRUPTIVE MOOD BEHAVIOR ASSESSMENT WORKSHEET

DATE _____

TOP 3 DISRUPTIVE PROBLEMS TODAY

○ _____

○ _____

○ _____

HE / SHE MADE ME

Behavioral observations that require continuous follow-up

SOLUTION DIAGRAM: _____

_____

_____

_____

Suggestions to do

Evaluation of applied treatment ideas

Overall assessment of disruptive mood behavior

☆ ☆ ☆ ☆ ☆

Weekly / Monthly Goals

BEHAVIORAL OBJECTIVES

♡ _____

♡ _____

♡ _____

PARENTAL GOALS

♡ _____

♡ _____

♡ _____

THERAPEUTIC OBJECTIVES

♡ _____

♡ _____

♡ _____

DISRUPTIVE MOOD BEHAVIOR ASSESSMENT WORKSHEET

DATE _____

TOP 3 DISRUPTIVE PROBLEMS TODAY

○ _____

○ _____

○ _____

SOLUTION DIAGRAM: _____

HE / SHE MADE ME

Behavioral observations that require continuous follow-up

_____

_____

_____

_____

Suggestions to do

Evaluation of applied treatment ideas

Overall assessment of disruptive mood behavior

☆ ☆ ☆ ☆ ☆

Weekly Monthly Goals

BEHAVIORAL OBJECTIVES

♡ _____

♡ _____

♡ _____

PARENTAL GOALS

♡ _____

♡ _____

♡ _____

THERAPEUTIC OBJECTIVES

♡ _____

♡ _____

♡ _____

DISRUPTIVE MOOD BEHAVIOR ASSESSMENT WORKSHEET

DATE _____

TOP 3 DISRUPTIVE PROBLEMS TODAY

○ _____

○ _____

○ _____

SOLUTION DIAGRAM: _____

HE / SHE MADE ME

Behavioral observations that require continuous follow-up

_____

_____

_____

Suggestions to do

Evaluation of applied treatment ideas

Overall assessment of disruptive mood behavior

☆ ☆ ☆ ☆ ☆

Weekly / Monthly Goals

BEHAVIORAL OBJECTIVES

♡ _____

♡ _____

♡ _____

PARENTAL GOALS

♡ _____

♡ _____

♡ _____

THERAPEUTIC OBJECTIVES

♡ _____

♡ _____

♡ _____

DISRUPTIVE MOOD BEHAVIOR ASSESSMENT WORKSHEET

DATE _____

TOP 3 DISRUPTIVE PROBLEMS TODAY

○ _____

○ _____

○ _____

SOLUTION DIAGRAM: _____

HE / SHE MADE ME

Behavioral observations that require continuous follow-up

_____

_____

_____

_____

Suggestions to do

Evaluation of applied treatment ideas

Overall assessment of disruptive mood behavior

☆ ☆ ☆ ☆ ☆

Weekly / Monthly Goals

BEHAVIORAL OBJECTIVES

♡ _____

♡ _____

♡ _____

PARENTAL GOALS

♡ _____

♡ _____

♡ _____

THERAPEUTIC OBJECTIVES

♡ _____

♡ _____

♡ _____

DISRUPTIVE MOOD BEHAVIOR ASSESSMENT WORKSHEET

DATE _____

TOP 3 DISRUPTIVE PROBLEMS TODAY

○ _____
○ _____
○ _____

SOLUTION DIAGRAM: _____

HE / SHE MADE ME

Behavioral observations that require continuous follow-up

_____

_____

_____

Suggestions to do

Evaluation of applied treatment ideas

Overall assessment of disruptive mood behavior

☆ ☆ ☆ ☆ ☆

Weekly / Monthly Goals

BEHAVIORAL OBJECTIVES

♡ _____

♡ _____

♡ _____

PARENTAL GOALS

♡ _____

♡ _____

♡ _____

THERAPEUTIC OBJECTIVES

♡ _____

♡ _____

♡ _____

DISRUPTIVE MOOD BEHAVIOR ASSESSMENT WORKSHEET

DATE _____

TOP 3 DISRUPTIVE PROBLEMS TODAY

○ _____

○ _____

○ _____

SOLUTION DIAGRAM: _____

HE / SHE MADE ME

Behavioral observations that require continuous follow-up

_____

_____

_____

_____

Suggestions to do

Evaluation of applied treatment ideas

Overall assessment of disruptive mood behavior

☆ ☆ ☆ ☆ ☆

Weekly Monthly Goals

BEHAVIORAL OBJECTIVES

♡ _____

♡ _____

♡ _____

PARENTAL GOALS

♡ _____

♡ _____

♡ _____

THERAPEUTIC OBJECTIVES

♡ _____

♡ _____

♡ _____

DISRUPTIVE MOOD BEHAVIOR ASSESSMENT WORKSHEET

DATE _____

TOP 3 DISRUPTIVE PROBLEMS TODAY

○ _____

○ _____

○ _____

HE / SHE MADE ME

Behavioral observations that require continuous follow-up

SOLUTION DIAGRAM: _____

_____

_____

_____

_____

Suggestions to do

Evaluation of applied treatment ideas

Overall assessment of disruptive mood behavior

☆ ☆ ☆ ☆ ☆

Weekly / Monthly Goals

BEHAVIORAL OBJECTIVES

- ♡ _____
- ♡ _____
- ♡ _____

PARENTAL GOALS

- ♡ _____
- ♡ _____
- ♡ _____

THERAPEUTIC OBJECTIVES

- ♡ _____
- ♡ _____
- ♡ _____

DISRUPTIVE MOOD BEHAVIOR ASSESSMENT WORKSHEET

DATE _____

TOP 3 DISRUPTIVE PROBLEMS TODAY

○ _____

○ _____

○ _____

HE / SHE MADE ME

Behavioral observations that require continuous follow-up

_____

_____

_____

_____

SOLUTION DIAGRAM: _____

Suggestions to do

Evaluation of applied treatment ideas

Overall assessment of disruptive mood behavior

☆ ☆ ☆ ☆ ☆

Weekly / Monthly Goals

BEHAVIORAL OBJECTIVES

♡ _____

♡ _____

♡ _____

PARENTAL GOALS

♡ _____

♡ _____

♡ _____

THERAPEUTIC OBJECTIVES

♡ _____

♡ _____

♡ _____

DISRUPTIVE MOOD BEHAVIOR ASSESSMENT WORKSHEET

DATE _____

TOP 3 DISRUPTIVE PROBLEMS TODAY

- ○ _____
- ○ _____
- ○ _____

HE / SHE MADE ME

Behavioral observations that require continuous follow-up

SOLUTION DIAGRAM: _____

_____

_____

_____

_____

Suggestions to do

Evaluation of applied treatment ideas

Overall assessment of disruptive mood behavior

☆ ☆ ☆ ☆ ☆

Weekly / Monthly Goals

BEHAVIORAL OBJECTIVES

♡ _____

♡ _____

♡ _____

PARENTAL GOALS

♡ _____

♡ _____

♡ _____

THERAPEUTIC OBJECTIVES

♡ _____

♡ _____

♡ _____

DISRUPTIVE MOOD BEHAVIOR ASSESSMENT WORKSHEET

DATE _____

TOP 3 DISRUPTIVE PROBLEMS TODAY

○ _____

○ _____

○ _____

SOLUTION DIAGRAM: _____

HE / SHE MADE ME

Behavioral observations that require continuous follow-up

_____

_____

_____

_____

Suggestions to do

Evaluation of applied treatment ideas

Overall assessment of disruptive mood behavior

☆ ☆ ☆ ☆ ☆

Weekly Monthly Goals

BEHAVIORAL OBJECTIVES

♡ _____

♡ _____

♡ _____

PARENTAL GOALS

♡ _____

♡ _____

♡ _____

THERAPEUTIC OBJECTIVES

♡ _____

♡ _____

♡ _____

DISRUPTIVE MOOD BEHAVIOR ASSESSMENT WORKSHEET

DATE _____

TOP 3 DISRUPTIVE PROBLEMS TODAY

○ _____

○ _____

○ _____

SOLUTION DIAGRAM: _____

HE / SHE MADE ME

Behavioral observations that require continuous follow-up

_____

_____

_____

_____

Suggestions to do

Evaluation of applied treatment ideas

Overall assessment of disruptive mood behavior

☆ ☆ ☆ ☆ ☆

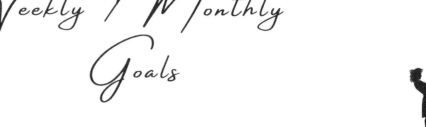

Weekly / Monthly Goals

BEHAVIORAL OBJECTIVES

♡ _____

♡ _____

♡ _____

PARENTAL GOALS

♡ _____

♡ _____

♡ _____

THERAPEUTIC OBJECTIVES

♡ _____

♡ _____

♡ _____

DISRUPTIVE MOOD BEHAVIOR ASSESSMENT WORKSHEET

DATE _____

TOP 3 DISRUPTIVE PROBLEMS TODAY

○ _____

○ _____

○ _____

SOLUTION DIAGRAM: _____

HE / SHE MADE ME

Behavioral observations that require continuous follow-up

_____

_____

_____

_____

Suggestions to do

Evaluation of applied treatment ideas

Overall assessment of disruptive mood behavior

☆ ☆ ☆ ☆ ☆

Weekly Monthly Goals

BEHAVIORAL OBJECTIVES

♡ _____

♡ _____

♡ _____

PARENTAL GOALS

♡ _____

♡ _____

♡ _____

THERAPEUTIC OBJECTIVES

♡ _____

♡ _____

♡ _____

DISRUPTIVE MOOD BEHAVIOR ASSESSMENT WORKSHEET

DATE _____

TOP 3 DISRUPTIVE PROBLEMS TODAY

○ _____

○ _____

○ _____

SOLUTION DIAGRAM: _____

HE / SHE MADE ME

Behavioral observations that require continuous follow-up

_____

_____

_____

_____

Suggestions to do

Evaluation of applied treatment ideas

Overall assessment of disruptive mood behavior

☆ ☆ ☆ ☆ ☆

Weekly / Monthly Goals

BEHAVIORAL OBJECTIVES

♡ _____

♡ _____

♡ _____

PARENTAL GOALS

♡ _____

♡ _____

♡ _____

THERAPEUTIC OBJECTIVES

♡ _____

♡ _____

♡ _____

DISRUPTIVE MOOD BEHAVIOR ASSESSMENT WORKSHEET

DATE _____

TOP 3 DISRUPTIVE PROBLEMS TODAY

○ _____

○ _____

○ _____

HE / SHE MADE ME

Behavioral observations that require continuous follow-up

_____

_____

_____

_____

SOLUTION DIAGRAM: _____

Suggestions to do

Evaluation of applied treatment ideas

Overall assessment of disruptive mood behavior

☆ ☆ ☆ ☆ ☆

Weekly Monthly Goals

BEHAVIORAL OBJECTIVES

♡ _____

♡ _____

♡ _____

PARENTAL GOALS

♡ _____

♡ _____

♡ _____

THERAPEUTIC OBJECTIVES

♡ _____

♡ _____

♡ _____

DISRUPTIVE MOOD BEHAVIOR ASSESSMENT WORKSHEET

DATE _____

TOP 3 DISRUPTIVE PROBLEMS TODAY

- ○ _____
- ○ _____
- ○ _____

SOLUTION DIAGRAM: _____

HE / SHE MADE ME

Behavioral observations that require continuous follow-up

_____

_____

_____

Suggestions to do

Evaluation of applied treatment ideas

Overall assessment of disruptive mood behavior

☆ ☆ ☆ ☆ ☆

Weekly / Monthly Goals

BEHAVIORAL OBJECTIVES

♡ _____

♡ _____

♡ _____

PARENTAL GOALS

♡ _____

♡ _____

♡ _____

THERAPEUTIC OBJECTIVES

♡ _____

♡ _____

♡ _____

DISRUPTIVE MOOD BEHAVIOR ASSESSMENT WORKSHEET

DATE _____

TOP 3 DISRUPTIVE PROBLEMS TODAY

○ _____

○ _____

○ _____

SOLUTION DIAGRAM: _____

HE / SHE MADE ME

Behavioral observations that require continuous follow-up

_____

_____

_____

_____

Suggestions to do

Evaluation of applied treatment ideas

Overall assessment of disruptive mood behavior

☆ ☆ ☆ ☆ ☆

Weekly Monthly Goals

BEHAVIORAL OBJECTIVES

♡ _____

♡ _____

♡ _____

PARENTAL GOALS

♡ _____

♡ _____

♡ _____

THERAPEUTIC OBJECTIVES

♡ _____

♡ _____

♡ _____

DISRUPTIVE MOOD BEHAVIOR ASSESSMENT WORKSHEET

DATE _____

TOP 3 DISRUPTIVE PROBLEMS TODAY

- ○ _____
- ○ _____
- ○ _____

SOLUTION DIAGRAM: _____

HE / SHE MADE ME

Behavioral observations that require continuous follow-up

_____

_____

_____

_____

Suggestions to do

Evaluation of applied treatment ideas

Overall assessment of disruptive mood behavior

☆ ☆ ☆ ☆ ☆

Weekly / Monthly Goals

BEHAVIORAL OBJECTIVES

♡ _____

♡ _____

♡ _____

PARENTAL GOALS

♡ _____

♡ _____

♡ _____

THERAPEUTIC OBJECTIVES

♡ _____

♡ _____

♡ _____

DISRUPTIVE MOOD BEHAVIOR ASSESSMENT WORKSHEET

DATE _____

TOP 3 DISRUPTIVE PROBLEMS TODAY

○ _____
○ _____
○ _____

SOLUTION DIAGRAM: _____

HE / SHE MADE ME

Behavioral observations that require continuous follow-up

_____

_____

_____

_____

Suggestions to do

Evaluation of applied treatment ideas

Overall assessment of disruptive mood behavior

☆ ☆ ☆ ☆ ☆

Weekly Monthly Goals

BEHAVIORAL OBJECTIVES

- ♡ _____
- ♡ _____
- ♡ _____

PARENTAL GOALS

- ♡ _____
- ♡ _____
- ♡ _____

THERAPEUTIC OBJECTIVES

- ♡ _____
- ♡ _____
- ♡ _____

DISRUPTIVE MOOD BEHAVIOR ASSESSMENT WORKSHEET

DATE _____

TOP 3 DISRUPTIVE PROBLEMS TODAY

○ _____

○ _____

○ _____

HE / SHE MADE ME

SOLUTION DIAGRAM: _____

Behavioral observations that require continuous follow-up

_____

_____

_____

_____

Suggestions to do

Evaluation of applied treatment ideas

Overall assessment of disruptive mood behavior

☆ ☆ ☆ ☆ ☆

Weekly / Monthly Goals

BEHAVIORAL OBJECTIVES

♡ _____

♡ _____

♡ _____

PARENTAL GOALS

♡ _____

♡ _____

♡ _____

THERAPEUTIC OBJECTIVES

♡ _____

♡ _____

♡ _____

DISRUPTIVE MOOD BEHAVIOR ASSESSMENT WORKSHEET

DATE _____

TOP 3 DISRUPTIVE PROBLEMS TODAY

○ _____

○ _____

○ _____

SOLUTION DIAGRAM: _____

HE / SHE MADE ME

Behavioral observations that require continuous follow-up

_____

_____

_____

_____

Suggestions to do

Evaluation of applied treatment ideas

Overall assessment of disruptive mood behavior

☆ ☆ ☆ ☆ ☆

Weekly / Monthly Goals

BEHAVIORAL OBJECTIVES

♡ _____

♡ _____

♡ _____

PARENTAL GOALS

♡ _____

♡ _____

♡ _____

THERAPEUTIC OBJECTIVES

♡ _____

♡ _____

♡ _____

DISRUPTIVE MOOD BEHAVIOR ASSESSMENT WORKSHEET

DATE _____

TOP 3 DISRUPTIVE PROBLEMS TODAY

○ _____

○ _____

○ _____

SOLUTION DIAGRAM: _____

HE / SHE MADE ME

Behavioral observations that require continuous follow-up

_____

_____

_____

Evaluation of applied treatment ideas

Suggestions to do

Overall assessment of disruptive mood behavior

☆ ☆ ☆ ☆ ☆

Weekly Monthly Goals

BEHAVIORAL OBJECTIVES

♡ _____

♡ _____

♡ _____

PARENTAL GOALS

♡ _____

♡ _____

♡ _____

THERAPEUTIC OBJECTIVES

♡ _____

♡ _____

♡ _____

DISRUPTIVE MOOD BEHAVIOR ASSESSMENT WORKSHEET

DATE _____

TOP 3 DISRUPTIVE PROBLEMS TODAY

○ _____

○ _____

○ _____

SOLUTION DIAGRAM: _____

HE / SHE MADE ME

Behavioral observations that require continuous follow-up

_____

_____

_____

_____

Suggestions to do

Evaluation of applied treatment ideas

Overall assessment of disruptive mood behavior

☆ ☆ ☆ ☆ ☆

Weekly / Monthly Goals

BEHAVIORAL OBJECTIVES

♡ _____

♡ _____

♡ _____

PARENTAL GOALS

♡ _____

♡ _____

♡ _____

THERAPEUTIC OBJECTIVES

♡ _____

♡ _____

♡ _____

DISRUPTIVE MOOD BEHAVIOR ASSESSMENT WORKSHEET

DATE _____

TOP 3 DISRUPTIVE PROBLEMS TODAY

○ _____

○ _____

○ _____

HE / SHE MADE ME

Behavioral observations that require continuous follow-up

_____

_____

_____

_____

SOLUTION DIAGRAM: _____

Suggestions to do

Evaluation of applied treatment ideas

Overall assessment of disruptive mood behavior

☆ ☆ ☆ ☆ ☆

Weekly / Monthly Goals

BEHAVIORAL OBJECTIVES

♡ _____

♡ _____

♡ _____

PARENTAL GOALS

♡ _____

♡ _____

♡ _____

THERAPEUTIC OBJECTIVES

♡ _____

♡ _____

♡ _____

DISRUPTIVE MOOD BEHAVIOR ASSESSMENT WORKSHEET

DATE _____

TOP 3 DISRUPTIVE PROBLEMS TODAY

○ _____

○ _____

○ _____

SOLUTION DIAGRAM: _____

HE / SHE MADE ME

Behavioral observations that require continuous follow-up

_____

_____

_____

_____

Suggestions to do

Evaluation of applied treatment ideas

Overall assessment of disruptive mood behavior

☆ ☆ ☆ ☆ ☆

Weekly Monthly Goals

BEHAVIORAL OBJECTIVES

♡ _____

♡ _____

♡ _____

PARENTAL GOALS

♡ _____

♡ _____

♡ _____

THERAPEUTIC OBJECTIVES

♡ _____

♡ _____

♡ _____

DISRUPTIVE MOOD BEHAVIOR ASSESSMENT WORKSHEET

DATE _____

TOP 3 DISRUPTIVE PROBLEMS TODAY

○ _____

○ _____

○ _____

SOLUTION DIAGRAM: _____

HE / SHE MADE ME

Behavioral observations that require continuous follow-up

_____

_____

_____

Suggestions to do

Evaluation of applied treatment ideas

Overall assessment of disruptive mood behavior

☆ ☆ ☆ ☆ ☆

Weekly / Monthly Goals

BEHAVIORAL OBJECTIVES

♡ _____

♡ _____

♡ _____

PARENTAL GOALS

♡ _____

♡ _____

♡ _____

THERAPEUTIC OBJECTIVES

♡ _____

♡ _____

♡ _____

DISRUPTIVE MOOD BEHAVIOR ASSESSMENT WORKSHEET

DATE _____

TOP 3 DISRUPTIVE PROBLEMS TODAY

○ _____

○ _____

○ _____

SOLUTION DIAGRAM: _____

HE / SHE MADE ME

Behavioral observations that require continuous follow-up

_____

_____

_____

_____

Suggestions to do

Evaluation of applied treatment ideas

Overall assessment of disruptive mood behavior

☆ ☆ ☆ ☆ ☆

Weekly / Monthly Goals

BEHAVIORAL OBJECTIVES

♡ _____
♡ _____
♡ _____

PARENTAL GOALS

♡ _____
♡ _____
♡ _____

THERAPEUTIC OBJECTIVES

♡ _____
♡ _____
♡ _____

DISRUPTIVE MOOD BEHAVIOR ASSESSMENT WORKSHEET

DATE _____

TOP 3 DISRUPTIVE PROBLEMS TODAY

○ _____

○ _____

○ _____

SOLUTION DIAGRAM: _____

HE / SHE MADE ME

Behavioral observations that require continuous follow-up

_____

_____

_____

_____

Suggestions to do

Evaluation of applied treatment ideas

Overall assessment of disruptive mood behavior

☆ ☆ ☆ ☆ ☆

Weekly Monthly Goals

BEHAVIORAL OBJECTIVES

♡ _____
♡ _____
♡ _____

PARENTAL GOALS

♡ _____
♡ _____
♡ _____

THERAPEUTIC OBJECTIVES

♡ _____
♡ _____
♡ _____

DISRUPTIVE MOOD BEHAVIOR ASSESSMENT WORKSHEET

DATE _____

TOP 3 DISRUPTIVE PROBLEMS TODAY

○ _____

○ _____

○ _____

HE / SHE MADE ME

Behavioral observations that require continuous follow-up

_____

_____

_____

_____

SOLUTION DIAGRAM: _____

Suggestions to do

Evaluation of applied treatment ideas

Overall assessment of disruptive mood behavior

☆ ☆ ☆ ☆ ☆

Weekly Monthly Goals

BEHAVIORAL OBJECTIVES

♡ _____

♡ _____

♡ _____

PARENTAL GOALS

♡ _____

♡ _____

♡ _____

THERAPEUTIC OBJECTIVES

♡ _____

♡ _____

♡ _____

DISRUPTIVE MOOD BEHAVIOR ASSESSMENT WORKSHEET

DATE _____

TOP 3 DISRUPTIVE PROBLEMS TODAY

○ _____

○ _____

○ _____

SOLUTION DIAGRAM: _____

HE / SHE MADE ME

Behavioral observations that require continuous follow-up

_____

_____

_____

_____

Suggestions to do

Evaluation of applied treatment ideas

Overall assessment of disruptive mood behavior

☆ ☆ ☆ ☆ ☆

Weekly Monthly Goals

BEHAVIORAL OBJECTIVES

♡ _____
♡ _____
♡ _____

PARENTAL GOALS

♡ _____
♡ _____
♡ _____

THERAPEUTIC OBJECTIVES

♡ _____
♡ _____
♡ _____

DISRUPTIVE MOOD BEHAVIOR ASSESSMENT WORKSHEET

DATE _____

TOP 3 DISRUPTIVE PROBLEMS TODAY

_____
○ _____
○ _____
○ _____

SOLUTION DIAGRAM: _____

HE / SHE MADE ME

Behavioral observations that require continuous follow-up

_____

_____

_____

_____

Suggestions to do

Evaluation of applied treatment ideas

Overall assessment of disruptive mood behavior

☆ ☆ ☆ ☆ ☆

Weekly Monthly Goals

BEHAVIORAL OBJECTIVES

♡ _____

♡ _____

♡ _____

PARENTAL GOALS

♡ _____

♡ _____

♡ _____

THERAPEUTIC OBJECTIVES

♡ _____

♡ _____

♡ _____

DISRUPTIVE MOOD BEHAVIOR ASSESSMENT WORKSHEET

DATE _____

TOP 3 DISRUPTIVE PROBLEMS TODAY

○ _____

○ _____

○ _____

SOLUTION DIAGRAM: _____

HE / SHE MADE ME

Behavioral observations that require continuous follow-up

_____

_____

_____

_____

Suggestions to do

Evaluation of applied treatment ideas

Overall assessment of disruptive mood behavior

☆ ☆ ☆ ☆ ☆

Weekly / Monthly Goals

BEHAVIORAL OBJECTIVES

♡ _____

♡ _____

♡ _____

PARENTAL GOALS

♡ _____

♡ _____

♡ _____

THERAPEUTIC OBJECTIVES

♡ _____

♡ _____

♡ _____

DISRUPTIVE MOOD BEHAVIOR ASSESSMENT WORKSHEET

DATE _____

TOP 3 DISRUPTIVE PROBLEMS TODAY

○ _____

○ _____

○ _____

SOLUTION DIAGRAM: _____

HE / SHE MADE ME

Behavioral observations that require continuous follow-up

_____

_____

_____

_____

Suggestions to do

Evaluation of applied treatment ideas

Overall assessment of disruptive mood behavior

☆ ☆ ☆ ☆ ☆

Weekly Monthly Goals

BEHAVIORAL OBJECTIVES

♡ _____

♡ _____

♡ _____

PARENTAL GOALS

♡ _____

♡ _____

♡ _____

THERAPEUTIC OBJECTIVES

♡ _____

♡ _____

♡ _____

DISRUPTIVE MOOD BEHAVIOR ASSESSMENT WORKSHEET

DATE _____

TOP 3 DISRUPTIVE PROBLEMS TODAY

○ _____

○ _____

○ _____

SOLUTION DIAGRAM: _____

HE / SHE MADE ME

Behavioral observations that require continuous follow-up

_____

_____

_____

_____

Suggestions to do

Evaluation of applied treatment ideas

Overall assessment of disruptive mood behavior

☆ ☆ ☆ ☆ ☆

Weekly Monthly Goals

BEHAVIORAL OBJECTIVES

♡ _____

♡ _____

♡ _____

PARENTAL GOALS

♡ _____

♡ _____

♡ _____

THERAPEUTIC OBJECTIVES

♡ _____

♡ _____

♡ _____

DISRUPTIVE MOOD BEHAVIOR ASSESSMENT WORKSHEET

DATE _____

TOP 3 DISRUPTIVE PROBLEMS TODAY

_____
○
_____
○
_____
○
_____

SOLUTION DIAGRAM: _____

HE / SHE MADE ME

Behavioral observations that require continuous follow-up

_____

_____

_____

_____

Suggestions to do

Evaluation of applied treatment ideas

Overall assessment of disruptive mood behavior

☆ ☆ ☆ ☆ ☆

Weekly Monthly Goals

BEHAVIORAL OBJECTIVES

♡ _____

♡ _____

♡ _____

PARENTAL GOALS

♡ _____

♡ _____

♡ _____

THERAPEUTIC OBJECTIVES

♡ _____

♡ _____

♡ _____

DISRUPTIVE MOOD BEHAVIOR ASSESSMENT WORKSHEET

DATE _____

TOP 3 DISRUPTIVE PROBLEMS TODAY

○ _____

○ _____

○ _____

SOLUTION DIAGRAM: _____

HE / SHE MADE ME

Behavioral observations that require continuous follow-up

_____

_____

_____

_____

Suggestions to do

Evaluation of applied treatment ideas

Overall assessment of disruptive mood behavior

☆ ☆ ☆ ☆ ☆

Weekly Monthly Goals

BEHAVIORAL OBJECTIVES

♡ _____

♡ _____

♡ _____

PARENTAL GOALS

♡ _____

♡ _____

♡ _____

THERAPEUTIC OBJECTIVES

♡ _____

♡ _____

♡ _____

DISRUPTIVE MOOD BEHAVIOR ASSESSMENT WORKSHEET

DATE _____

TOP 3 DISRUPTIVE PROBLEMS TODAY

○ _____

○ _____

○ _____

SOLUTION DIAGRAM: _____

HE / SHE MADE ME

Behavioral observations that require continuous follow-up

_____

_____

_____

_____

Suggestions to do

Evaluation of applied treatment ideas

Overall assessment of disruptive mood behavior

☆ ☆ ☆ ☆ ☆

Weekly Monthly Goals

BEHAVIORAL OBJECTIVES

♡ _____

♡ _____

♡ _____

PARENTAL GOALS

♡ _____

♡ _____

♡ _____

THERAPEUTIC OBJECTIVES

♡ _____

♡ _____

♡ _____

DISRUPTIVE MOOD BEHAVIOR ASSESSMENT WORKSHEET

DATE _____

TOP 3 DISRUPTIVE PROBLEMS TODAY

○ _____

○ _____

○ _____

SOLUTION DIAGRAM: _____

HE / SHE MADE ME

Behavioral observations that require continuous follow-up

_____

_____

_____

_____

Suggestions to do

Evaluation of applied treatment ideas

Overall assessment of disruptive mood behavior

☆ ☆ ☆ ☆ ☆

Weekly / Monthly Goals

BEHAVIORAL OBJECTIVES

♡ _____

♡ _____

♡ _____

PARENTAL GOALS

♡ _____

♡ _____

♡ _____

THERAPEUTIC OBJECTIVES

♡ _____

♡ _____

♡ _____

DISRUPTIVE MOOD BEHAVIOR ASSESSMENT WORKSHEET

DATE _____

TOP 3 DISRUPTIVE PROBLEMS TODAY

○ _____

○ _____

○ _____

SOLUTION DIAGRAM: _____

HE / SHE MADE ME

Behavioral observations that require continuous follow-up

_____

_____

_____

_____

Suggestions to do

Evaluation of applied treatment ideas

Overall assessment of disruptive mood behavior

☆ ☆ ☆ ☆ ☆

Weekly Monthly Goals

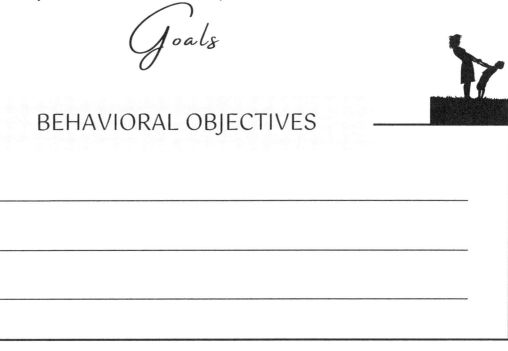

BEHAVIORAL OBJECTIVES

♡ _____

♡ _____

♡ _____

PARENTAL GOALS

♡ _____

♡ _____

♡ _____

THERAPEUTIC OBJECTIVES

♡ _____

♡ _____

♡ _____

DISRUPTIVE MOOD BEHAVIOR ASSESSMENT WORKSHEET

DATE _____

TOP 3 DISRUPTIVE PROBLEMS TODAY

SOLUTION DIAGRAM: _____

○ _____

○ _____

○ _____

HE / SHE MADE ME

Behavioral observations that require continuous follow-up

_____

_____

_____

Suggestions to do

Evaluation of applied treatment ideas

Overall assessment of disruptive mood behavior

☆ ☆ ☆ ☆ ☆

Weekly Monthly Goals

BEHAVIORAL OBJECTIVES

♡ _____

♡ _____

♡ _____

PARENTAL GOALS

♡ _____

♡ _____

♡ _____

THERAPEUTIC OBJECTIVES

♡ _____

♡ _____

♡ _____

DISRUPTIVE MOOD BEHAVIOR ASSESSMENT WORKSHEET

DATE _____

TOP 3 DISRUPTIVE PROBLEMS TODAY

○ _____

○ _____

○ _____

SOLUTION DIAGRAM: _____

HE / SHE MADE ME

Behavioral observations that require continuous follow-up

_____

_____

_____

_____

Suggestions to do

Evaluation of applied treatment ideas

Overall assessment of disruptive mood behavior

☆ ☆ ☆ ☆ ☆

Weekly Monthly Goals

BEHAVIORAL OBJECTIVES

♡ _____

♡ _____

♡ _____

PARENTAL GOALS

♡ _____

♡ _____

♡ _____

THERAPEUTIC OBJECTIVES

♡ _____

♡ _____

♡ _____

DISRUPTIVE MOOD BEHAVIOR ASSESSMENT WORKSHEET

DATE _____

TOP 3 DISRUPTIVE PROBLEMS TODAY

_____
○ _____
○ _____
○ _____

SOLUTION DIAGRAM: _____

HE / SHE MADE ME

Behavioral observations that require continuous follow-up

_____

_____

_____

_____

Suggestions to do

Evaluation of applied treatment ideas

Overall assessment of disruptive mood behavior

☆ ☆ ☆ ☆ ☆

Weekly Monthly Goals

BEHAVIORAL OBJECTIVES

♡ _____

♡ _____

♡ _____

PARENTAL GOALS

♡ _____

♡ _____

♡ _____

THERAPEUTIC OBJECTIVES

♡ _____

♡ _____

♡ _____

DISRUPTIVE MOOD BEHAVIOR ASSESSMENT WORKSHEET

DATE _____

TOP 3 DISRUPTIVE PROBLEMS TODAY

○ _____

○ _____

○ _____

SOLUTION DIAGRAM: _____

HE / SHE MADE ME

Behavioral observations that require continuous follow-up

_____

_____

_____

_____

Suggestions to do

Evaluation of applied treatment ideas

Overall assessment of disruptive mood behavior

☆ ☆ ☆ ☆ ☆

Weekly Monthly Goals

BEHAVIORAL OBJECTIVES

♡ _____

♡ _____

♡ _____

PARENTAL GOALS

♡ _____

♡ _____

♡ _____

THERAPEUTIC OBJECTIVES

♡ _____

♡ _____

♡ _____

DISRUPTIVE MOOD BEHAVIOR ASSESSMENT WORKSHEET

DATE _____

TOP 3 DISRUPTIVE PROBLEMS TODAY

○ _____

○ _____

○ _____

SOLUTION DIAGRAM: _____

HE / SHE MADE ME

Behavioral observations that require continuous follow-up

_____

_____

_____

_____

Suggestions to do

Evaluation of applied treatment ideas

Overall assessment of disruptive mood behavior

☆ ☆ ☆ ☆ ☆

Weekly Monthly Goals

BEHAVIORAL OBJECTIVES

♡ _____

♡ _____

♡ _____

PARENTAL GOALS

♡ _____

♡ _____

♡ _____

THERAPEUTIC OBJECTIVES

♡ _____

♡ _____

♡ _____

DISRUPTIVE MOOD BEHAVIOR ASSESSMENT WORKSHEET

DATE _____

TOP 3 DISRUPTIVE PROBLEMS TODAY

○ _____

○ _____

○ _____

SOLUTION DIAGRAM: _____

HE / SHE MADE ME

Behavioral observations that require continuous follow-up

_____

_____

_____

_____

Suggestions to do

Evaluation of applied treatment ideas

Overall assessment of disruptive mood behavior

☆ ☆ ☆ ☆ ☆

Weekly / Monthly Goals

BEHAVIORAL OBJECTIVES

♡ _____

♡ _____

♡ _____

PARENTAL GOALS

♡ _____

♡ _____

♡ _____

THERAPEUTIC OBJECTIVES

♡ _____

♡ _____

♡ _____

DISRUPTIVE MOOD BEHAVIOR ASSESSMENT WORKSHEET

DATE _____

TOP 3 DISRUPTIVE PROBLEMS TODAY

○ _____

○ _____

○ _____

SOLUTION DIAGRAM: _____

HE / SHE MADE ME

Behavioral observations that require continuous follow-up

_____

_____

_____

_____

Suggestions to do

Evaluation of applied treatment ideas

Overall assessment of disruptive mood behavior

☆ ☆ ☆ ☆ ☆

Weekly / Monthly Goals

BEHAVIORAL OBJECTIVES

♡ _____

♡ _____

♡ _____

PARENTAL GOALS

♡ _____

♡ _____

♡ _____

THERAPEUTIC OBJECTIVES

♡ _____

♡ _____

♡ _____

DISRUPTIVE MOOD BEHAVIOR ASSESSMENT WORKSHEET

DATE _____

TOP 3 DISRUPTIVE PROBLEMS TODAY

○ _____

○ _____

○ _____

SOLUTION DIAGRAM: _____

HE / SHE MADE ME
_____

Behavioral observations that require continuous follow-up

_____

_____

_____

_____

Suggestions to do

Evaluation of applied treatment ideas

Overall assessment of disruptive mood behavior

☆ ☆ ☆ ☆ ☆

Weekly / Monthly Goals

BEHAVIORAL OBJECTIVES

♡ _____

♡ _____

♡ _____

PARENTAL GOALS

♡ _____

♡ _____

♡ _____

THERAPEUTIC OBJECTIVES

♡ _____

♡ _____

♡ _____

Made in the USA
Monee, IL
15 December 2022